HISTORY IN DEPTH

THE ARAB-ISRAELI CONFLICT

S.J. Perkins

Head of History, Grey Court School, Richmond, Surrey

M
MACMILLAN
EDUCATION

For Hannah

First published 1987
Reprinted 1987

Published by
MACMILLAN EDUCATION LTD
Houndmills, Basingstoke, Hampshire RG21 2XS
and London
Companies and representatives
throughout the world

Printed in Hong Kong

British Library Cataloguing in Publication Data
Perkins, S. J.
The Arab—Israeli conflict.—(History in depth)
1. Jewish—Arab relations—To 1917
2. Jewish—Arab relations—1917—
I. Title   II. Series
956   DS119.7
ISBN 0—333—40919—1

Cover illustration shows Jerusalem
by courtesy of Sheridan Photo Library

CONTENTS

Acknowledgements

The author and publishers wish to thank the following who have kindly given permission for the use of copyright material:

Middle East Journal for material from 'Visions of the Return: The Palestine Arab Refugees in Arabic Poetry and Art' by Tibawi, MEJ, 17, No. 4, 1963.

The publishers have made every effort to trace the copyright holders, but if they have inadvertently overlooked any, they will be pleased to make the necessary arrangements at the first opportunity.

The author and publishers wish to acknowledge, with thanks, the following photographic sources:

Associated Press pp 57 bottom, 61; BBC Hulton Picture Library/Bettmann Archive p 32; Beth Hatefutsoth, Museum of the Jewish Diaspora p 7; BIPAC pp 13 bottom, 30, 38; Camera Press pp 8, 31, 49 left, 52 bottom; Fifth of June Society p 24; Institute of Contemporary History and Weiner Library Ltd p 26 top; *Jerusalem Post* p 45; Mansell Collection pp 10, 22; Middle East Collection, St Antony's College, Oxford p 23; Photo Source Ltd pp 5 top, 5 centre, 12 right, 35, 49 right, 53, 55; PLO p 52 top; Popperfoto pp 5 bottom, 20, 25, 29, 34, 39; *Punch* p 42; Roger-Viollet p 11; Ullstein p 26 bottom; UNRWA pp 48, 59 (photographs by George Nehmeh), 51 (photograph by Munir Nasr); Zionist Archives, Jerusalem pp 12 left, 12 bottom, 13 top.

The map on page 49 is based on one from Martin Gilbert's *The Arab–Israeli Conflict – its history in maps*, Weidenfeld & Nicolson, 1985.

PREFACE

The study of history is exciting, whether in a good story well told, a mystery solved by the judicious unravelling of clues, or a study of the men, women and children whose fears and ambitions, successes and tragedies make up the collective memory of mankind.

This series aims to reveal this excitement to pupils through a set of topic books on important historical subjects from the Middle Ages to the present day. Each book contains four main elements: a narrative and descriptive text, lively and relevant illustrations, extracts of contemporary evidence, and questions for further thought and work. Involvement in these elements should provide an adventure which will bring the past to life in the imagination of the pupil.

Each book is also designed to develop the knowledge, skills and concepts so essential to a pupil's growth. It provides a wide, varying introduction to the evidence available on each topic. In handling this evidence, pupils will increase their understanding of basic historical concepts such as causation and change, as well as of more advanced ideas such as revolution and democracy. In addition, their use of basic study skills will be complemented by more sophisticated historical skills such as the detection of bias and the formulation of opinion.

The intended audience for the series is pupils of eleven to sixteen years: it is expected that the earlier topics will be introduced in the first three years of secondary school, while the nineteenth and twentieth century topics are directed towards first examinations.

IN THE BEGINNING

Munich, 1972

Joseph Romano

Moshe Weinberg

Munich massacre – this apartment was used by the Israeli athletes

At 4.30 a.m. on 5 September 1972 guards at the Olympic Village, Munich, took little notice as eight men in training kit climbed the perimeter fence. There was nothing unusual in this. Many athletes came back this way from a night on the town. The men, however, carried large bags which betrayed a sinister purpose. Perhaps the guards did not pay them the attention they deserved.

That same morning, Moshe Weinberg, a wrestler with the Israeli team, returned late. He had seen a performance of *Fiddler on the Roof* and had eaten in an Israeli restaurant. As he made his way to Block No. 31, where the Israeli team were housed, he ran into the tracksuited figures. These were no athletes. They were members of the Palestinian terrorist organisation, Black September, and they were armed with Kalashnikov automatic rifles. They attacked Weinberg but he resisted, and in the panic that followed he was shot trying to allow the escape of another athlete. In the end, nine Israeli athletes were captured and held hostage. Some escaped but two men, Weinberg and a weightlifter called Joseph Romano, lay dead.

Just after 5 a.m. the terrorists made their demands. By 9 a.m. they wanted the release of 200 Palestinian prisoners held in Israel, otherwise the hostages would be shot. The Israeli government was contacted but refused to bargain. The German authorities must not give in to the terrorists' demands, they said. The deadline was extended to midday as the Germans negotiated for more time. They offered the gunmen safe passage, money and even a good time with 'beautiful Munich blondes'. They were not interested. As further deadlines expired a deal was struck. The kidnappers said they were willing to fly to Cairo.

At 10.15 p.m. helicopters took the terrorists and their hostages to the Fürstenfeldbruck military airport where a Lufthansa aeroplane was waiting on the runway. Two of the terrorists jumped down to check the aeroplane. Everything was ready but there was no crew. As they moved back, German marksmen opened fire. One of the terrorists was hit, but the other took cover by the helicopters, which still held the hostages. For a while there was no shooting. Then at 1.05 a.m. the gun battle was renewed. A grenade was thrown into one of the helicopters and the nine Israeli hostages were blown up. As the drama unfolded it became clear that all the hostages were dead, together with five of the terrorists.

Three days later the Israelis launched a reprisal air strike over Syria and Lebanon in which up to 500 people died.

The Arab-Israeli conflict

The killing of the Israeli athletes at the 1972 Munich Olympics by the Palestinian group, Black September, highlights very clearly the conflict between Jews and Arabs. The Munich massacre also demonstrated that the conflict had been 'exported'. Terrorism had become international. People throughout the world were shocked and outraged. Since then nothing appears to have changed. If anything, people have become used to reading newspaper reports from the Middle East of hijackings, car-bombings, attacks on embassies, raids on villages and political assassinations. Television news programmes regularly flash pictures of Middle Eastern conflicts into our living rooms. Why is this? Why is there so much conflict between Arabs and Jews and in the Middle East generally? This book will examine these questions.

The issues raised are important. For example, a permanent large-scale war in the Middle East would threaten vital oil supplies to the West. And because the superpowers (Russia and the United States) have become involved in the region, the conflict threatens to destroy the world through nuclear warfare. The search for a peaceful and lasting settlement in the Middle East is one of the world's most pressing problems.

To understand how the conflict has arisen we must begin by considering the history, culture, customs and claims to Palestine of both Jews and Arabs.

The Jews
The Jews claim Palestine as their homeland on the basis of the story in the Old Testament which tells how they came to settle there. The area, known as Judea, was conquered by the Romans in 63 BC.

In AD 135 the Romans put down a Jewish revolt and plundered the city of Jerusalem. After this, Jews were forbidden to live there. Judea was wiped from the map and the region became known as Syria Palestina. A few devout Jews stayed, but most were scattered throughout the lands of the Roman Empire. In this diaspora or dispersion the Jews were soon to experience suffering and persecution.

In the lands where they settled, Jews lived as minorities. Here they preserved their Jewishness through their traditions and, most of all, their religion. Their strange ways and clothes did not endear them to local Christian communities who felt threatened by this alien presence. People began to blame the Jews for misfortunes and to charge them with fantastic crimes. For example, on 26 May 1171, 50 Jews of the city of Blois in France were burnt alive after allegations that a young Jewish boy had thrown a Christian boy into a river.

The 'blood libel': a 15th century woodcut showing Jews extracting blood from a child's body

Stories circulated that Jews were killing Christians to use their blood for Jewish rituals. Further horrors followed as Jews were massacred throughout the Christian lands of Europe, accused of these foul deeds. From time to time laws were passed that prevented Jews from entering Christian occupations and owning property. The role of moneylending, regarded as sinful by Christians, was the only profitable occupation left open to them, but this did not increase their popularity.

The Warsaw ghetto in the early 1940s. Dead bodies are being wheeled out after an uprising

Some countries expelled their Jews; for example, they were forced to leave England in 1292, France in 1306 and Spain in 1492. In other countries they were confined to ghettoes – separate quarters walled off from the rest of the community. Squalid, bleak and cramped, the ghettoes offered Jews little hope of a better life. In 1795 a visitor described the Jewish ghetto in Frankfurt:

> *Imagine a long street flanked by houses five to six storeys high. Imagine these houses with rear wings, and these with still other rear wings, the courtyards barely large enough to allow some daylight to enter. Every corner of each house is full to the rooftop with narrow rooms and chambers, and into them, tier on tier, are crowded ten thousand persons who consider themselves fortunate when they can leave their caves and catch a breath of air in their dank and dirty street.... Then you have an approximate notion of the Jews' quarter.*
> Quoted in Werner Keller's book, *The Post-Biblical History of the Jews*, 1971

Such places could be found in towns all over Europe. In them the Jews physically deteriorated – they became pale, sickly, bowed and sunken-eyed. Small wonder that people saw them as strangely repulsive. In Russia by the nineteenth century conditions were even worse. Here all Jews were restricted to an area known as the 'Pale of Settlement', where they lived in abject poverty.

The Arabs
What is your view of an Arab? One historian, Peter Mansfield, wrote:

To most westerners the word Arab . . . seemed to conjure up a picture of a sheikh in flowing robes, brandishing an outdated rifle as he urged his camel across the sand dunes to attack a neighbouring encampment.

Peter Mansfield: *The Arabs*, 1976

Newspapers and films often depict the Arab in romantic and exotic terms. These Western images conceal how Arabs view their own sense of past greatness. Another historian, Professor Gibb, points out:

The Arab sense of bygone splendour is superb. One cannot begin to understand the modern Arab if one lacks a perspective feeling for this.

Quoted in Peter Mansfield's book, *The Arabs*, 1976

Who, then, are the Arabs and what have been their achievements? In biblical times most Arabs lived in the Arabian Desert and followed a nomadic and tribal existence. Arabs had always lived in Palestine, but after the Romans drove out the Jews in AD 135 they dwelt there increasingly. The year AD 570 signified momentous changes for the Arab world. In that year the prophet Mohammed was born. He brought a new religion, Islam, to Arab people and a way of life which involved total submission to Allah. Arabs believe that Mohammed was the last and the greatest of the prophets of God.

In AD 632 the great prophet died. Arab armies spread the new faith. In the centuries that followed, Arab influence extended from the pyramids to the Punjab. During this 'Golden Age' Arab civilisation flowered. The great libraries and schools of Baghdad became the centre of learning for poets, scholars and philosophers of all nationalities. Arabs achieved remarkable advances in medicine, mathematics and science.

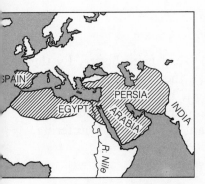

The Arab Empire in the 8th century AD

Towards the end of the eleventh century, however, the Arab Empire fell into decline. By the sixteenth century the Arabs were ruled by the Turks. During this period of Ottoman supremacy the Arabs were not treated harshly. Arabs and Turks shared the same Islamic faith and the Turks let the Arabs have a say in their own affairs. Arabs, however, look back on this period as their 'Dark Age'. Living in the Ottoman Empire, the Arabs fell behind the West in learning, technology and wealth. Towards the end of the nineteenth century many Arabs blamed their backwardness on Turkish rule.

Questions

1 What claims do the Jews have on Palestine?

2 What claims do the Arabs have on Palestine?

3 Is it possible to say which is the stronger claim?

THE SEEDS OF STRIFE, 1880-1920

Pogrom

On 1 March 1881, Tsar Alexander II of Russia was returning from a military parade. Suddenly, a terrific explosion rocked the carriage in which he was travelling. Shaken, but unhurt, the Tsar stepped down to speak to his bodyguard when a second bomb fatally wounded him. A Jewish woman was implicated in the assassination plot and rumours spread of a Jewish conspiracy. The mob was soon to exact a terrible revenge, sacking and burning Jewish quarters in towns all over Russia. This was the phenomenon of pogrom (from the Russian verb *pogromit*, meaning 'to destroy'). In the years that followed, pogroms would break out over and over again.

Theodor Herzl and Zionism

A pogrom in Kiev. Note the reaction of the authorities. Why do you think such attacks were seemingly condoned?

In the countries of Western Europe, Jews had fared better. By the 1880s they had gained more freedom than their counterparts in the East. Many were educated and well-to-do, becoming wealthy as a result of the new industrial developments of the age. For many others, however, the machine age brought hardship and suffering,

particularly in times of economic depression when unemployment rose. Those lucky enough to have jobs received low wages for long hours of hard, tedious manual labour. The uncertainty of the times led people to look for a scapegoat. The Jews, with their distinctive dress, religion, language and customs, were obvious targets. People blamed Jews for the shortcomings of society. A popular anti-Jewish slogan ran:

What the Jew believes is all the same;
It's the race that's all the filth and shame.

One man who viewed this situation with despair was Theodor Herzl. In 1891 he became Paris correspondent for the Austrian newspaper *Neue Freie Presse*. In France, Herzl confronted the Jewish question in the notorious Dreyfus affair. Alfred Dreyfus, a French army captain and a Jew, was accused of spying for Germany. He was tried, convicted and sentenced to life imprisonment. Herzl attended the public ceremony where Dreyfus, protesting his innocence, was stripped of his rank. Outside, a mob howled 'Death! Death to the Jews!'

For Herzl such events put the Jewish question into sharp focus. He decided to express his views in a book called *The Jewish State*, and its publication in 1896 marked the beginning of modern political Zionism:

I think the Jewish question is no more a social than a religious one; it is a national question; we are a people — one people. We have honestly tried everywhere to merge our societies in which we live and to preserve our religion. We are not permitted to do this. In countries

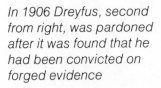

In 1906 Dreyfus, second from right, was pardoned after it was found that he had been convicted on forged evidence

Right: Anti-Semitic cartoon. The Knights of Zionism: 'Well, dear coreligionist – will you follow us to Zion?' The coreligionist: 'Nu, what could one nebbish do in Zion? But I'll buy from you.'

Viennese cartoon: 'The biggest Jew alive'

Theodor Herzl

where we have lived for centuries we are still looked down on as strangers. . . . Everything tends in fact to the same conclusion which is clearly put in that classic Berlin phrase 'Juden raus' ('Out with the Jews'). I shall now put the question in the briefest possible form: are we to get out now and where to? The whole plan is in essence perfectly simple. Let us be given sovereignty over part of the world big enough to satisfy the rightful needs of a nation; the rest we shall manage for ourselves.

Theodor Herzl: *Der Judenstaat*, 1896

The Basel Congress

The following year, in 1897, Herzl organised the First Zionist Congress, in Basel, Switzerland. From 16 countries, 206 delegates arrived. After many speeches the Congress adopted an official programme known as the Basel Declaration. The main aim of Zionism

Above: *The Basel Congress, 1897. Delegates were asked to wear 'black formal attire'. Why do you think black was preferred to light-coloured suits?*

Right: *Degania, the first kibbutz*

was defined as 'to create for the Jewish people a homestead in Palestine secured by public law'. Ways of achieving this aim were laid down. When Herzl closed the Congress there were scenes of euphoria. From all round the hall came shouts of 'Next year in Jerusalem' — a prayer said frequently by Jews in exile.

Following the Basel Congress, Herzl worked furiously to promote the Zionist cause. He established a weekly Zionist newspaper, *Dïe Welt*, and negotiated with the Sultan of Turkey to allow Jewish settlement in Palestine. When Herzl died in 1904, Chaim Weizmann became leader of the Zionist movement. The early years of his leadership saw further violent pogroms in Eastern Europe. A second wave of immigrants came to Palestine, so that by 1914 the Jewish population had increased to about 85 000 compared to an Arab population of 650 000. The new settlers were rugged pioneers who brought the idea of collective agricultural settlements, known as kibbutzim, the first of which was established at Degania in 1909. The Arabs

13

watched the growing number of Jewish immigrants with alarm and, ominously, skirmishes between Arabs and Jews took place where Arabs had been ousted from the land.

Assignment

Write a speech of the kind Herzl might have made to the Basel Congress, outlining why the Jews should have a homeland in Palestine. You will also need to refer back to the section headed 'The Jews' in Chapter 1.

Arab nationalism

At the same time as Zionism was taking root in Europe, a movement to free Arabs from their Turkish overlords developed. Progress, however, was gradual. One of the problems facing Arabs was lack of unity. Some blamed Turkish rule. Others thought the Caliph, the leader of the Islamic world, should be an Arabian Arab living in Mecca, rather than the Turkish Sultan.

In 1908 a revolution by 'Young Turks' deposed the Sultan, Abdul Hamid II. These Turkish patriots hoped to halt the decline of their empire with a stronger brand of Turkish nationalism — a policy known as Ottomanisation. The teaching of the Turkish language in schools and the wearing of the fez became compulsory. Proud Arabs bitterly resented this interference in their established customs and traditions. 'Rather death than the fez,' they cried, and violent clashes between Turks and Arabs ensued. Arab secret societies were formed and in 1913 the First Arab National Congress was held. A year later a Manifesto of Arab Nationalism was published from Cairo:

> *Arise, O ye Arabs! Unsheathe the sword from the scabbard. Do not let an oppressive tyrant who has only disdain for you remain in your country; cleanse the country from those who show their enmity to you, to your race and to your language....O ye Arabs! You all dwell in one place, you speak one language, so be also one nation and one land.*

While many Arabs believed in such an appeal there was no sign of open revolt against the Turks.

Assignment

Write an appeal of the kind an Arab might have made at the First National Congress, explaining why Arabs should be free of Turkish rule. Also refer back to the section headed 'The Arabs' in Chapter 1.

European involvement

By the first decade of the twentieth century European countries had become increasingly involved in the Middle East. The Suez Canal, completed in 1869, provided Britain with a vital link to its Far Eastern trading empire. To protect this route, Great Britain had taken control of Egypt in 1882. France, too, had interests in this region. Algeria and Tunisia were French colonies and there was considerable French influence in Syria and Lebanon. Germany attempted to gain a foothold in the Middle East by befriending Turkey. In a policy known as 'Drang nach Osten', German money flooded into Turkey and helped to build the Baghdad railway.

When oil was found in large quantities in Persia in 1908, the Middle East became of even greater interest to the European countries, especially Great Britain whose naval fleet was being converted from coal to oil-fired ships. These developments in the Middle East would soon be of great significance as tensions in Europe drew the major powers into war.

Britain's promise to the Arabs

On 5 November 1914 Turkey declared war on Britain, France and Russia and so joined the Central Powers, Germany and Austria-Hungary, in a world war that was to last for four years. As a result of Turkey's declaration, Britain entered into negotiations with Sharif Hussein of Mecca, the recognised leader of the Arab world. Sir Henry McMahon, the British High Commissioner in Egypt, represented Britain in these negotiations.

Using the evidence: the Hussein–McMahon correspondence

On 14 July 1915 Hussein wrote to McMahon asking Britain to support Arab independence in the areas marked 1–8 on the map.

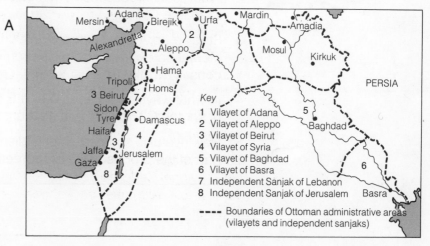

A

Key
1 Vilayet of Adana
2 Vilayet of Aleppo
3 Vilayet of Beirut
4 Vilayet of Syria
5 Vilayet of Baghdad
6 Vilayet of Basra
7 Independent Sanjak of Lebanon
8 Independent Sanjak of Jerusalem

- - - Boundaries of Ottoman administrative areas (vilayets and independent sanjaks)

On 24 October McMahon replied stating:

B   ...*Great Britain is prepared to recognise and support the independence of the Arabs in all the regions within the limits demanded by the Sharif of Mecca....*

In the same letter McMahon did make certain modifications to that pledge in an 'exclusion clause' which said:

C   ...*portions of Syria lying to the west of the districts of Damascus, Homs, Hama and Aleppo, cannot be said to be purely Arab, and should be excluded from the limits demanded...[by Sharif Hussein].*

Historians have interpreted this 'exclusion clause'. This is what two of them have said:

D   *The geographical limits of the Arab area to become independent were loosely described and made no reference to Palestine.... Palestine west of the Jordan would fall under this exclusion.*
   Michael Comay: *Zionism and Israel*, 1976

E   *Since Palestine lay to the south of Damascus, the people of that area not unnaturally concluded that their independence would follow an Allied victory in the First World War.*
   Jonathan Dimbleby: *The Palestinians*, 1979

In 1937 Sir Henry McMahon wrote:

F   *I feel it is my duty to state that it was not intended by me in giving this pledge to Sharif Hussein to include Palestine in the area in which Arab independence was promised.*
   Sir Henry McMahon, *The Times*, 1937

1   What promise does McMahon make to the Arabs in source B?

2   What reason does McMahon give for excluding certain areas in source C?

3   Study map A and source C. Which modern area do you think McMahon excluded from his promise? (You may need to consult an atlas.)

4   In what ways do sources D and E differ in their interpretation of source C? How do you account for this difference?

5   How useful is source F in establishing whether Palestine was part of the proposed British agreement with the Arabs?

The Sykes-Picot agreement

At the same time as the Hussein–McMahon negotiations were taking place, Britain was also making a secret agreement with France. The map below shows the results of the discussions between Sir Mark Sykes and M. Georges Picot, which centred on the partition of the old Ottoman Empire in the event of an Allied victory.

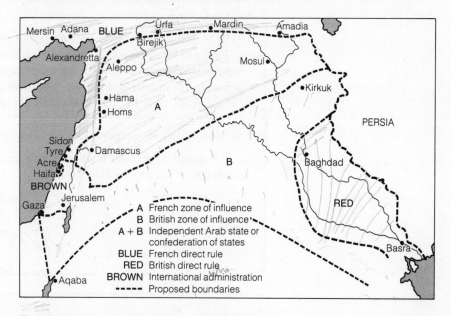

The Sykes-Picot agreement, 1916

Questions

Compare the map showing the Sykes-Picot agreement with the Hussein–McMahon correspondence.

1 How far does the Sykes-Picot agreement contradict Britain's promise to the Arabs?

2 What provision was made for Palestine in the McMahon–Hussein letters and the Sykes-Picot agreement?

British support for Zionism

Throughout World War I the aims of the Zionists had been of less immediate importance than those of the Arabs. This changed in 1917. Despite the fact that only 56 000 Jews lived in Palestine compared to a total Arab population of 700 000, Lord Balfour, the British Foreign Secretary, wrote the following letter to Lord Rothschild, a leading British Zionist:

Foreign Office,
November 2nd, 1917.

Dear Lord Rothschild,

I have much pleasure in conveying to you, on behalf of His Majesty's Government, the following declaration of sympathy with Jewish Zionist aspirations which has been submitted to, and approved by, the Cabinet:

"His Majesty's Government view with favour the establishment in Palestine of a national home for the Jewish people, and will use their best endeavours to facilitate the achievement of this object, it being clearly understood that nothing shall be done which may prejudice the civil and religious rights of existing non-Jewish communities in Palestine, or the rights and political status enjoyed by Jews in any other country."

I should be grateful if you would bring this declaration to the knowledge of the Zionist Federation.

Y. sing

Arthur James Balfour

Questions

1 How did Balfour aim to help the Jews?

2 Who were the 'non-Jewish communities'? Why might they resent this description?

3 Does Balfour give any indication of how the civil and religious rights of the 'non-Jewish communities' were to be protected?

Exactly why Britain issued the Balfour Declaration is not entirely clear. In 1917 the war in Europe dragged on. A fresh initiative was needed. Perhaps the government hoped that support for Zionism would influence Jews in America to push their government into war. Certainly, in the event of an Allied victory it would be of great strategic benefit to Britain to know that a government near Suez was on its side. Whatever the motives, Balfour later revealed where Britain's sympathies lay in a memorandum to the Cabinet in 1919:

In Palestine we do not propose even to go through the form of consulting the wishes of the present inhabitants of the country. . . . the Four Great Powers are committed to Zionism. . . . And Zionism, be it right or wrong, good or bad, is rooted in agelong traditions, in present needs, in future hopes, of far profounder import than the desires and prejudices of the 700,000 Arabs who now inhabit that ancient land.

Quoted in Doreen Ingrams' book, *Palestine Papers, 1917–22*, 1972

Using the evidence: a consistent policy?

Look back through the chapter and compare Britain's Middle-Eastern agreements. Consider how a Jew and an Arab might react to them and how the British might justify them, then copy out and complete the chart below. In particular, consider how each agreement dealt with the question of Palestine.

Agreement	Reaction/Justification		
	Arab reaction	Jewish reaction	British justification
The McMahon–Hussein correspondence			
The Sykes–Picot agreement			
The Balfour Declaration			

How coherent and consistent do you think Britain's Middle-Eastern policy was during the war years?

3

NO PEACE IN PALESTINE, 1920-36

*The Jaffa riots, 1921.
Jewish homes are burnt by
an Arab mob*

By 1921 the sea port of Jaffa had already developed its famous export trade of oranges. With its closely packed alleys and mixed groups of waterfront workers it looked much like any other Arab coastal town. On closer inspection, however, the easy-going appearance belied deeper tensions, for Jaffa had become the central point of Jewish immigration into Palestine. On 1 May 1921 the simmering unrest suddenly erupted into violent riots as Jews and Arabs attacked each other with great brutality. When the fighting stopped, 200 Jews and 120 Arabs lay dead or wounded.

Using the evidence: the Jaffa riots of 1921

A British Commission of Inquiry, led by Sir Thomas Haycraft, considered the nature and causes of the violence. Study the following extracts.

A   The storming of the Zionist Immigration Hostel, Jaffa, by an Arab mob.

We are satisfied from the evidence of Reverend A.C. Martin of the London Jews Society, who saw much of what happened on the opposite side of the main street, that the [Arab] police in the street broke through the door and led part of the mob into the yard. They broke into the ground floor of the main building and into the other buildings. Men who sought refuge by running into the street were beaten to death by the crowd. Others were killed inside the courtyard.

B   [The Arabs saw]...the beginnings of industrial strife, previously unknown in the country; they saw strikes and labour demonstrations, which filled their conservative minds with alarm; they read leaflets...in which people were invited to participate in class war, and to promote anarchy and social upheaval....

anarchy: lawlessness

Several witnesses have referred to the manner in which strings of [Jewish] young men and women, in free and easy attire, would perambulate the streets arm in arm, singing songs, holding up the traffic and generally conducting themselves in a manner at variance with Arab ideas of decorum.

decorum: dignified behaviour

1   According to source A, who led the assault on the Jewish Immigration Hostel?

2   'Source A is based on the evidence of an eye witness and is therefore reliable.' Discuss this statement.

3   a) How might a historian seek to check the reliability of source A?
    b) What difficulties do you think a historian might find in establishing exactly what happened in the Jaffa riots?

4   According to source B, what ideas and attitudes did the Jews bring which the Arabs found offensive?

5   How does source B help to explain the violence described in source A?

The British Mandate

The riots in Jaffa came as a shock not only to the Jews but also to the British. Since the break up of the Turkish Empire at the end of World War I, Britain had held the Mandate of Palestine. This meant that it was Britain's responsibility to rule Palestine until it was able to form its own government. The Mandate also required Britain to work with the Zionists to help set up a national home for the Jews in Palestine. In 1922 this position was confirmed by the League of Nations:

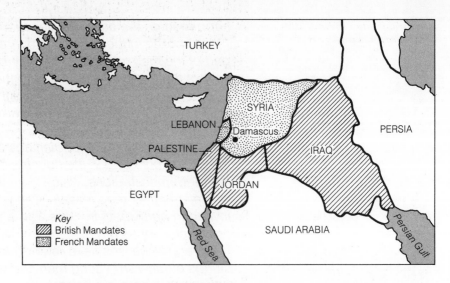

...The administration of Palestine, while ensuring that the rights and position of other sections of the population are not prejudiced, shall facilitate Jewish immigration under suitable conditions, in co-operation with the Jewish Agency, [and] close settlement by the Jews on the land....

Punch *cartoon, June 1922:* 'The half-promised land.' Why was it 'half-promised'?

Young Jewish immigrants transformed the land

Social unrest

After the Jaffa riots, the British authorities continued to support Jewish immigration in the 1920s. Most of the new arrivals settled on the kibbutzim. David Horowitz, one of the pioneers in the 1920s, recalls some of the problems they faced:

We arrived here in 1920 and settled on top of a hill above the Sea of Galilee. There was no road to this place. You could reach it only by mule or by foot and [it was] completely isolated from the outer world by the difficulty of communication. Foodstuffs were brought by mule and here we lived, 26 boys and girls who came directly from a completely different middle-class atmosphere and surroundings . . . . [We] lived on the verge of starvation [under] very difficult physical conditions. . . .[We all lived] in two rooms of a wooden shack . . . four girls in one room, 22 boys in the other. Bed was near bed with very little space between and in the day people did very hard physical manual work and in the night. . .people sat down on the rocks and talked about the basic problems of life.

David Horowitz, speaking on television in 1977

Despite such tremendous hardships the kibbutzim made an important contribution to the Zionist movement in the 1920s. Young immigrants worked together to develop their settlements and through their zeal, enterprise and skill the land was transformed out of all recognition. Young settlers such as David Ben-Gurion saw the development of the land as essential to implanting the Jewish national home. As he himself said: 'Every kibbutz, every factory, every house is a step towards the fulfilment of that aim.' Jewish hospitals, banks, schools and industries sprang up. Sports were organised in which Jewish songs and flag waving produced deep feelings of nationalism.

In this Jewish scheme of things, however, there was no place for the Arab. Arabs were expelled from the land when Jewish settlers

Haifa

Sea of Galilee

Mediterranean Sea

Nazareth

Tel Aviv

Jaffa

Jerusalem

Bethlehem

Gaza

Dead Sea

EGYPT

Key

Main areas of Jewish settlement in the 1920s

took over and Jewish employers were shunned if they took on Arab labour. To the Arabs it appeared that the Jews were taking over their country. As we saw on page 21, many Arabs found the European values brought by the Jews offensive and distasteful. Mohammed Al-Aamiry remembers the different lifestyle brought by the Jews:

I remember our renting (we had a house of two storeys)...the lower storey to a Jewish/Polish family and I remember women behaved in the normal European way and [for] one thing they were scantily dressed...and to us young men that was unusual...of course for older people it was detested...while of course Arab women were fully dressed up and some of them were veiled...if you go to the sea there you can see European Jewish ladies with a swimming dress.

Mohammed Al-Aamiry, speaking on television in 1977

And Carl Raswan put into words the feelings of the Arab villagers who had seen the effect the Jews had on the traditional Arab way of life:

Money is God [in Tel Aviv]. Must all Palestine become one day like this, including the Holy City of Jerusalem? Tel Aviv is an ulcer eating into our own country. If it is what the Jews want to make Palestine, I wish my children dead. We do not mind poverty, but we weep when our peace is taken away. We lived a modest and contented life, but what shall we do if our children grow up to ape the noisy ways of these new people?

Quoted in H. Sachar's book, *A History of Israel*, 1976

Palestinian leaders protesting against the Balfour Declaration, 1925

The Wailing Wall, Jerusalem, is a holy shrine to both Jews and Arabs. To the Jews it is a place of pilgrimage, the last remains of the holy temple of Jerusalem. The Arabs call the wall the Burak, the name of the prophet Mohammed's horse. It is from here that he is thought to have embarked on his journey to heaven. In 1928 Jews started to change religious customs by bringing in a partition screen. This angered the Arabs who claimed that they were changing accepted practice.

It was a basic clash of cultures. The temperature rose among the Arab communities as Jewish immigration continued, reaching 160 000 by 1930. In August 1929 riots broke out in Jerusalem. This time 133 Jews and 116 Arabs were killed. The British White Paper that reported on these and other disturbances throughout Palestine gave some measure of support to the Arabs and suggested that Jewish immigration and land sales should be restricted. Any hope of this was soon to be dashed by events in Europe.

Question

Who had the right to administer the holy places?
Discuss this in class, then write a paragraph explaining your views.

Anti-Semitism in Europe

In the early hours of 10 November 1938, in Leipzig, the Nazis began a campaign of violence against the Jews which was unparalleled in history. Nazis broke into Jewish buildings, looting and burning Jewish property. Hundreds of Jewish shop windows were smashed and the streets were showered with broken glass. The three synagogues of Leipzig were set on fire and gutted beyond repair. The emergency services made no attempt to save them. Events such as these were not confined to Leipzig. On the same day, in Frankfurt, Cologne, Berlin and other German cities, similar orgies of anti-Jewish violence took place. In the end a total of 91 Jews lay dead and over 20 000 were arrested and taken to concentration camps.

25

Kristallnacht *(the night of broken glass) – a planned onslaught on Jewish life throughout Germany*

Below: *Two Germans accused of breaking Nazi laws forbidding sexual intercourse with Jews. They are forced to wear humiliating placards. Hers says: 'At this place I am the greatest swine: I take Jews and make them mine!' His declares: 'As a Jewish boy I always take German girls up to my room!'*

To Adolf Hitler, the leader of Germany's ruling Nazi Party, such persecution was sweet. In his book *Mein Kampf* Hitler described Jews as *untermenschen* (sub-humans) and identified them as the corrupters of the nation. When he came to power in 1933 Hitler had set about purging Germany of this 'racial disease'. Initially, Jews were barred from the professions, from sport and from the arts and later that year Hitler introduced anti-Semitic teaching in the schools. Soon,

prominent notices saying 'Jews not wanted here' were displayed in restaurants and hotels and Jewish shops were boycotted. In 1935 Hitler passed the infamous Nuremberg Laws which forbade marriage or sexual intercourse between Jews and Aryans (non-Jewish Germans).

Arab resistance

The million or so Palestinian Arabs were not much concerned with the plight of European Jews. However, when the ports of Palestine became crammed with boatloads of European Jews seeking refuge in their country, the Arabs took greater notice. In 1935 alone, the year of the Nuremberg Laws, 62 000 Jews arrived. The Arab nightmare of a Jewish state on their soil seemed to be coming true. In Arab eyes Britain did nothing to stop the rising tide of Jewish immigration and was therefore responsible for their misfortune. Ahram Zuayter, one of the Arab leaders in Nablus, recalls the Arab view of the British during this period:

The rate of Jewish immigration to Palestine, 1931–5	
Year	Number of immigrants
1931	4 075
1932	9 553
1933	30 327
1934	42 359
1935	61 854

> *Our message was simple. During the period of the Mandate the British should gradually have enabled us to move towards independence. That was supposed to be the goal of the Mandate. But it was clear the real goal was different. It was to establish a Jewish state on our ruins, to uproot the Arabs from their country. That was how we felt, that they were going to replace us with a Jewish state.*
>
> *For this reason the British were the cause of our catastrophe, and the catastrophe was Zionism. So we asked the people, 'Who is your first enemy?' 'Britain.' 'The second enemy?' 'Zionism.' 'Why?' 'Because Britain is responsible. Britain protects them and persecutes us.'*

Quoted in Jonathan Dimbleby's book, *The Palestinians*, 1979

Assignment

Imagine it is 1936 and you have been asked to write a newspaper article on the problem of Palestine. In your article explain the Arab, Jewish and British viewpoint, analysing how the problem has developed since Britain took over the Mandate of Palestine. You should also consider some possible solutions. For instance, what could be done for European Jews facing persecution if they were not to go to Palestine? Use the sources and information in this chapter, and any other relevant material. Include a headline and illustrate your article if you wish.

4 ISRAEL: 'A DIFFICULT BIRTH', 1936-48

Colonel Orde Wingate liked to scratch his naked body in public with a toothbrush. His methods, not to mention his personal habits, were unorthodox. Perhaps it was this very unpredictability which made him such a feared military genius. By 1938 Wingate had taken 'unofficial' charge of the Haganah, the Jewish defence force.

Since 1936 the Arabs had been waging guerilla war against the British. Now Wingate was taking his young Jewish settlers on a night raid against the Arab village of Hamita. For the eight-man squad, it had been a long and tiring trek through rough terrain. At last they had arrived. It was 3 a.m. Wingate positioned his men around the outskirts of the village and disappeared into the stillness of the night. Suddenly a shot rang out followed by a burst of gunfire. By the time Wingate returned five Arabs had been killed and four captured. Leonard Moseley, a British journalist, continues the story giving some insight into Wingate's methods of interrogation:

> He said in Arabic: 'You have arms in this village. Where have you hidden them?'
>
> The Arabs shook their heads and protested ignorance. Wingate reached down and took some sand and grit from the ground; he thrust it into the mouth of the first Arab and pushed it down his throat until he choked and puked.
>
> 'Now,' he said, 'Where have you hidden the arms?'
>
> Still they shook their heads. Wingate turned to one of the Jews and, pointing to the coughing and spluttering Arab, said: 'Shoot this man'.
>
> The Jew looked at him questioningly and hesitated. Wingate said in a tense voice: 'Did you hear? Shoot him!'
>
> The Jew shot the Arab. The others stared for a moment in stupefaction at the dead body at their feet.
>
> The boys from Hamita were watching in silence.
>
> 'Now speak,' said Wingate. They spoke.
>
> Leonard Moseley: *Gideon Goes to War*, 1955

The Arab rebellion, 1936–9

Since 1936 Palestine had been in a state of open rebellion as Arab groups took up arms in the hills, attacking British soldiers and property as well as Jewish settlements. There was a lull in the conflict as another British Royal Commission inquired into the problem.

The first Arab 'terrorists', 1938

When it reported in 1937, Lord Peel's Commission concluded:

The situation in Palestine has now reached deadlock. We cannot — in Palestine as it is now — both concede the Arab claim to self government and secure the establishment of the Jewish national home.

As the map on this page shows, the bold plan put forward by the Royal Commission was the partition of Palestine into separate Jewish and Arab states. While the Zionists accepted this as a basis for discussion, the Arabs felt bewildered and betrayed when they heard that the British government intended to carve up their native land. The Arabs recharged their guns and prepared to fight to the death. They stepped up guerilla attacks. The British responded by resorting to their own terror tactics — they made indiscriminate arrests, took hostages and used torture, hangings and collective fines to suppress the Arabs. By 1939 the Arab rebellion had been crushed.

Ironically, just as British troops in Palestine had quelled the Arabs, the British government was, yet again, about to change its policy. War clouds loomed over Europe and the British could not afford to have 20 000 troops pinned down in Palestine. Moreover, Western technology depended increasingly on oil and the Suez Canal remained of vital strategic importance as the gateway to the East. Arab friendship would be vital in the coming war. It was with these considerations in mind that the British government reversed its policy on Palestine. The MacDonald Report of 1939 stated:

It is proposed to establish within 10 years 'an independent Palestine State'... in which Arabs and Jews combine in government....

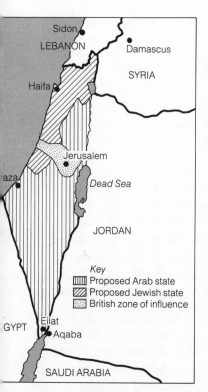

The Peel partition plan, 1937

29

Jews demonstrating in Jerusalem against the 1939 White Paper

For each of the next five years a quota of 10,000 Jewish immigrants will be allowed.

After the period of five years no further Jewish immigration will be permitted.

The 1937 Peel Commission had infuriated the Arabs; now the 1939 MacDonald Report infuriated the Jews.

The Nazi legacy

On 29 April 1945, US Corporal Bill Sanders was one of the first of the Allied forces to enter Dachau concentration camp. He recalls the scene that greeted him:

carloads: wagons

We turned left and there was a trainload of dead . . . 39 carloads as it turned out, and we counted approximately 2,500 bodies in them. The bottoms of the cars were covered with what looked like rags and it turned out to be bodies . . . some with clothing on and some naked, all starved to death. Of course, the smell of the bodies from the cars and possibly from the camp was quite overwhelming.

Bill Sanders, speaking on television in 1985

As the Allied forces liberated the Nazi concentration camps, including Auschwitz, Belsen and Dachau, the full, shuddering horror of the holocaust became apparent. On a scale of savagery difficult to imagine, 25 million people, six million of them Jews, had been exterminated. Hitler's delirious anti-Semitism had reached a new fury of frenzy during the war years. Survivors of the death camps spoke of torture, barbaric medical experiments, arbitrary mass

Genocide: six million Jews perished in the holocaust

exterminations in the gas chambers and starvation. The cameras of men like George Stephens whirred to show piles of emaciated bodies, 15 metres high, left to rot because the Nazis had run out of fuel to burn them. A new word, genocide, entered the dictionary.

Not unnaturally, a wave of sympathy went out to Jewish survivors, now refugees in Europe, who had nowhere to go. To many Jews it seemed that they had been hounded and slaughtered since time immemorial. After the war they began to demand a state of their own where they could be free from persecution. Noah Kliegner, a French Jew who survived Auschwitz, had no doubt about this:

> *Well, I was in Auschwitz when I realised that the only hope of survival for the Jews would be a state of our own, a country where we could live and work, a country that could protect us. Of course I didn't really believe that I would survive Auschwitz, but should I survive I decided I should be a very dedicated Zionist.*
>
> Noah Kliegner, speaking on television in 1985

Noah Kliegner joined the Haganah.

The politics of power

Added to the chorus of Zionists demanding a state of their own in Palestine came the most powerful voice of all, that of the President of the United States, Harry Truman. After the war Truman put pressure on Britain to admit 100 000 Jewish refugees into Palestine. How had this come about? Why did the United States decide to support Zionism?

31

During the war years the Zionists had been fairly active in enlisting American support for their cause. In May 1942, at the Biltmore Hotel, New York, Ben-Gurion organised a World Zionist Congress where he persuaded many wealthy American Jews to help the Zionists fight for a state in Palestine. When the war ended, Truman adopted the Biltmore Programme, declaring: 'I am sorry, gentlemen, but I have to answer to hundreds of thousands who are anxious for the success of Zionism: I do not have hundreds of thousands of Arabs among my constituents.'

Despite American pressure to admit the refugees, Ernest Bevin, the British Foreign Secretary, rejected the idea. He suggested that the Jewish refugees should resettle in Europe. Bevin feared that if Britain opened the floodgates to Jewish immigration, civil war between Jew and Arab would break out in Palestine. Furthermore, Bevin wished to build a new relationship with the Arab world. The importance of oil and the Suez Canal were vital factors, but Britain also hoped to build military bases in the Middle East. The Arab League (a league of independent Arab states, formed in 1945) did not want the Jews in Palestine either. 'Why should they come to our country?' the Arabs inquired. Britain, however, had emerged from the war economically weak and enfeebled. In 1946 food rationing was still in force and Britain was dependent on economic aid from America to help revive the economy. Christopher Mayhew, at that time a Junior Foreign Office Minister, recalls the way in which the United States put pressure on Britain:

Chicago, 1947. Jewish youth organisations picketing the British Embassy to protest against Britain's closed door policy in Palestine. Note the swastika on the Union Jack

I remember in Bevin's absence once I had to see the American Ambassador and he had a message from the President...that [he] wished to repeat his urgent and earnest request to admit immediately 100,000 Jewish refugees into Palestine...and I said...that the Secretary of State's view was that this was simply a recipe for war. Well, the Ambassador...simply said very deliberately that the President believes that if Mr Bevin accedes to his request that would help Britain's friends in Congress get through the latest appropriations of British aid, which is how a diplomat says...I mean there was bread rationing in Britain at the time...you do what we want or you go hungry.

Christopher Mayhew, speaking on television in 1985

Jewish terrorism

Just before noon on 22 July 1946 a truck containing milk churns drove up to the kitchen entrance of the King David Hotel, Jerusalem. Men in Arab dress began to unload their cargo and roll their milk churns into the Regency Café next to the kitchen. Little did anyone realise that the Arabs were members of Irgun, a Jewish terrorist group, and the milk churns contained high explosives. The King David Hotel, which housed the British Military Headquarters, had elaborate security above ground, but Irgun intelligence had discovered passageways running underneath the hotel. Irgun took control of the café. The milk churns were positioned. Menachem Begin, the leader of Irgun, continues the story:

It was now 12.15. Gideon (the Commander of the Assault Unit) was counting the minutes....Each minute seemed like a day. 12.31, 32. Zero hour drew near. Gideon grew restless. The half hour was almost up. 12.37...suddenly the whole town seemed to shudder. There had been no mistake....As the BBC put it – the entire wing of a huge building was cut off as with a knife.

Menachem Begin, *The Revolt*, 1951

Irgun's most spectacular plan, to blow up the King David Hotel, had been successful. Eighty-eight people (73 Britons and Arabs, as well as 15 Jews) died in the carnage.

Jewish terrorist acts such as these reached their height in 1946–7. During these years the Stern Gang, another Jewish group, and Irgun blew up radio and power stations, mined roads and raided military camps, killing soldiers in their beds. On one occasion they left two army sergeants hanging from a eucalyptus tree. Such acts were designed to pressurise the British into giving up their Mandate and allowing the Zionists to declare the State of Israel. Between 1945 and 1948, 338 British subjects met brutal deaths as a result of Jewish terrorism. This had a profound impact in Britain:

Jewish terrorists wanted by the British

Since each of the 338 was killed in a personal way, either singly with bullets or in a small group with a bomb, their deaths made as much impact on British public opinion, perhaps more impact, than the heavier British casualties of the Second World War, which were endured with fortitude and resolution. The 338, it seemed, had died quite unnecessarily. Political pressure to bring the killings to a halt was therefore all the stronger.

Nicholas Bethell, *The Palestine Triangle*, 1979

Propaganda

Despite Jewish terrorism Britain continued to refuse entry to Jewish refugees. In response, the Zionists stepped up their terror campaign and continued organising the entry of illegal immigrants to Palestine. Boats overloaded with Jewish refugees from Europe arrived at the ports of Palestine only to be turned back by the British. In the case of the ship *Exodus*, the newsreels showed the victims of Nazism

The ship Theodor Herzl *arriving in Palestine in 1947. What does the banner say? Why do you think this kind of propaganda had such a powerful effect on world opinion?*

The UN partition plan, 1947

Key
Proposed Arab state
Proposed Jewish state
International zone around Jerusalem

which it carried being returned to Germany. In fact, the whole incident had been deliberately arranged by the Zionists, who ensured that cameramen and newspaper reporters were aboard to record the scene. As the Arab historian Walid Al-Kayyali has stated:

This was the kind of battle the British simply could not win... because even if they intercepted these ships there were film crews and reporters on the ships that then transmitted an image of Britain as preventing survivors of the refugee camps from reaching the only shores of salvation. The main purpose of Zionist stategy...and it is a tribute and insight into their stategy...was to force Britain to give up the Mandate.

Walid Al-Kayyali, speaking on television in 1977

'Not a clean game'

Early in 1947 the war-weary British, facing Arab threats, Jewish terrorism and increasing criticism from the United States, decided to hand over the problem of Palestine to the United Nations. Throughout that summer, UN delegates went to Palestine to consider the problem. In September, they recommended that Palestine should be partitioned into separate Jewish and Arab states. Although the Zionists accepted this proposal, it was rejected by Britain and the Arabs. Britain said partition meant war. Eventually the partition scheme went to the vote when the full General Assembly convened in November 1947. The vote went in favour of partition, but it is clear that some member nations were subject to American strong-arm tactics:

President Truman warned one of his secretaries that he would demand a full explanation if nations which normally lined up with

the United States failed to do so on Palestine. Governments...were swayed by the most unorthodox arguments. The Firestone Tyre and Rubber Company, with plantations in Liberia, brought pressure to bear on the Liberian Government. It was hinted to Latin American delegates that their vote for partition would greatly increase their chances of a pan-American road project....
David Hirst, *The Gun and the Olive Branch*, 1977

As one Arab dryly remarked, it was 'not a clean game'. He added: 'The United Nations has no jurisdiction to partition Palestine against the wishes of its inhabitants.'

Question

Should the United Nations have partitioned Palestine into separate Jewish and Arab states? Make a list of arguments for and against partition.

Towards a state

The decision of the United Nations angered the Arabs who saw an outside body dissect their country. The Jews, too, were not completely satisfied with the proposed boundaries of the new state. Palestine became the scene of looting and bloodshed as Arab and Jewish groups attacked each other. The British, who still held the Mandate, did nothing but protect themselves. In the event, law and order in Palestine broke down completely. The Palestinians attacked Jewish convoys, bombed buildings and blockaded the road to Jerusalem. Jews carried out raids on Arab villages and spread terror. One of the worst atrocities took place at Deir Yassin, where the Arab civilian population was slaughtered by Irgun. During this period many Arabs fled from Palestine in fear of their lives.

A state is born

On 14 May 1948 the last British soldier left Palestine. The British Mandate was at an end. That same day the State of Israel was proclaimed. It had been a difficult birth. Many Jews feared Israel would not survive infancy as the combined Arab armies prepared to 'drive the Jews into the sea'.

Questions

1   Draw a time-line showing the main events in the formation of Israel, starting with the Arab rebellion in 1936.

2 The table below gives some factors that influenced Britain's decision to give up its Mandate of Palestine. Copy out the table and beside each factor say how important you think it was, and why.

Factors	Importance	Reasons (say what evidence supports your argument)
The holocaust		
American support for Zionism/ Britain's decline as a world power		
Jewish terrorism		
Propaganda		
The role of the United Nations		

3 In relation to Question 2, does any one factor alone explain why Britain gave up its Mandate? Explain your answer carefully.

A STATE OF WAR

David Ben-Gurion reading Israel's Declaration of Independence

At 4 p.m. on 14 May 1948 Ben-Gurion declared the new State of Israel with these words:

> *On 29 November 1947 the United Nations passed a resolution calling for the establishment of a Jewish State in Eretz-Israel... this recognition by the United Nations of the right of the Jewish people to establish their state is irrevocable.*

The following day troops from five neighbouring Arab states entered Israel determined to wipe out the fledgling state. Initially, things looked bleak for the Israeli defenders who were poorly equipped. Despite this the Arabs were unable to push home their overwhelming advantage in manpower and weapons. Personalities clashed in the Arab ranks and tactics conflicted. Meanwhile, the Israelis received new rifles from Czechoslovakia. Eventually, the Arabs were driven back on all fronts. The map on this page shows the final cease-fire lines which were agreed in February 1949.

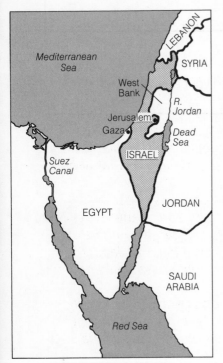

Israel – cease-fire lines, 1949

Using the evidence: the origins of the Palestinian refugee problem

During 1948–9 more than 700 000 Palestinians left their homeland and settled in refugee camps in neighbouring Arab states. The reasons for the Palestinian flight are hotly disputed.

A   The Arab version

> *On 9 April 1948 a Zionist force that included elements from the Irgun led by Menachem Begin; the Stern Gang led by Yitzhak Shamir; and the 'mainstream' Haganah [the embryonic Israeli army], attacked the peaceful Palestinian*

The Palestinian flight into exile, 1948–9. The reasons for the exodus are bitterly disputed

Arab village of Deir Yassin near Jerusalem and in cold blood murdered 154 men, women and children, mutilating many of the bodies. The plan was to frighten the rest of the Palestinian population into leaving to avoid the same fate, which they did in their thousands....Thousands of Palestinians who fled during the confusion and terror of the War (of Independence) were prevented from returning to their homes by Israel.

PLO pamphlet, *History of Palestine*, 1984

B   The Israeli version

On 14 May 1948 the British left, and the Arab armies invaded the country. Already, by that time, hundreds of thousands of Palestine Arabs had left their homes and had become refugees as a result of the fighting that had taken place in the country....When the regular Arab armies joined the fighting and full-scale war ensued, the number of refugees swelled.

...The responsibility for the fact that Arabs became refugees must lie with those who...perpetrated the aggression...against the State of Israel. Large numbers of the refugees left the country at the call of the Arab leaders, who told them to get out so that the Arab armies could get in....

dissident: disagreeing with the government

Arab representatives stressed the tragedy of Deir Yassin, where civilian Arabs were murdered by a Jewish dissident group... it is historically incorrect to state that the exodus of the Arab refugees was due to this incident.

Mrs Golda Meir, UN statement on the refugee problem, 1961

1 Why, according to source **A**, did the Palestinian population leave?

2 Why, according to source **B**, did the Palestinians leave?

3 Why do you think there is this difference of interpretation?

4 How might a historian go about checking the accuracy of each version? Which parts of sources **A** and **B** do you think would be most difficult to corroborate?

5 'Sources that contradict each other on the same subject are of little use to the historian.'
Do sources **A** and **B** prove this statement is correct?

Suez

The Arab defeat in the 1948 Palestine War was a humiliating blow to proud Arabs. One man who had fought bravely, however, was an Egyptian army officer, Gamal Abdel Nasser. After the war Nasser grew to despise the Egyptian king, Farouk, who seemed more interested in his own extravagant lifestyle than in the welfare of his subjects. In 1952, Nasser masterminded a revolution of 'Free Officers' which installed General Neguib as the new President of Egypt. Farouk was exiled in disgrace. Two years later Nasser became President. He was determined to improve the lot of the ordinary Egyptian. He introduced land reforms which restricted holdings to 80 hectares. To develop the economy, Nasser planned a great dam across the Nile at Aswan, which would provide hydroelectric power.

Nasser's other priority was to rid Egypt of British interference. Nasser said: 'Foreign invaders occupied our land. They built huge arsenals, terrorised the Egyptian people and sapped the national will.' In September 1954 Nasser reached an agreement with Britain on the evacuation of British troops. In return Britain hoped Nasser would join the Baghdad Pact which was being arranged as a defence against Russian Communism. Nasser, however, preferred neutrality. He also believed that all Arab countries should be free from foreign interference. Throughout the Arab world Cairo Radio's 'Voice of the Arabs' attacked the British as 'colonialist bloodsuckers'. As a result, many in the West regarded Nasser with suspicion.

Nasser, meanwhile, faced problems in the Gaza Strip where many Palestinians lived in squalid refugee camps. Since 1949 Arab groups known as fedayeen or self-sacrificers had attacked Israeli settlements in numerous border raids. In February 1955 Israel launched a reprisal raid into Gaza which destroyed the Egyptian army headquarters and killed a number of their soldiers. This angered Nasser.

He turned to the West for weapons. When Western leaders slammed the door in his face, Nasser was driven 'straight into the arms of Moscow'. In the autumn of 1955 Russian-made weapons and aeroplanes began to arrive in Egypt. The West was dismayed.

In 1955 Nasser was also seeking aid for the Aswan Dam project. In December, the United States, Britain and the World Bank agreed to finance it. The ink barely had time to dry, however, before the Western Powers were having second thoughts. Sir Anthony Eden, the British Prime Minister, detested Nasser and likened him to Hitler. In May 1956 Nasser upset the United States when he formally recognised Communist China. In July, the aid for the Aswan Dam was withdrawn. Britain and the United States hoped this would topple Nasser — but Nasser had other ideas.

On 26 July, before a vast crowd in Alexandria, Nasser made a broadcast to the nation. Adopting the earthy language of the people, Nasser spoke of the Suez Canal, which was jointly owned by Britain and France. He told the nation:

We dug the canal with our lives, our skulls, our bones, our blood...
120,000 [Egyptian] workers... died in forced labour on the canal.

Then Nasser announced his plan to nationalise the Suez Canal:

Today, O Citizens, with the annual income of the Suez Canal
amounting to...$100 million a year...we shall not look to the $70
million of American aid....
   Now, while I am talking to you, brothers of yours, sons of Egypt,
are rising up to direct the canal company and undertake its operation
...they are taking over the Egyptian Canal Company, not the
foreign Canal Company!

Nasser said the Western owners could 'die of their fury'. The Egyptians were delirious with joy. In Britain, Eden was furious. Nasser, he declared, had 'his thumb on our windpipe'. Eden wanted to teach Nasser a lesson. Thus Nasser's actions brought together the 'angry powers', Britain, France and Israel, who all had grievances against Egypt. At a secret meeting at Sèvres, near Paris, on 22—24 October, representatives of the three countries agreed on a joint plan to overthrow Nasser. Israel would invade Sinai and move in on the Canal Zone. Britain would then issue an ultimatum requesting Israel and Egypt to withdraw 16 kilometres either side of the canal. Eden knew that Nasser could not agree to this and so would give Britain the pretext to use military force — the so-called 'police action'. The map and chart on page 42 show how this was carried out.

In Britain opinion had been divided over Eden's action, but it was world condemnation that led to the withdrawal of British and French troops. The Russians threatened to attack Britain with missiles (although many regarded this as a mask for Russia's own brutal suppression of the Hungarian rebellion). More effectively, the

The Suez War, 1956

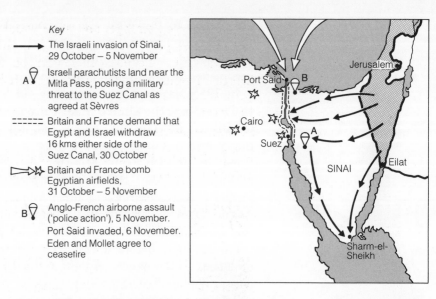

Key

→ The Israeli invasion of Sinai, 29 October – 5 November

Ⓐ Israeli parachutists land near the Mitla Pass, posing a military threat to the Suez Canal as agreed at Sèvres

====== Britain and France demand that Egypt and Israel withdraw 16 kms either side of the Suez Canal, 30 October

▷※ Britain and France bomb Egyptian airfields, 31 October – 5 November

Ⓑ Anglo-French airborne assault ('police action'), 5 November. Port Said invaded, 6 November. Eden and Mollet agree to ceasefire

United States stopped Britain receiving oil from its only other source, Latin America. In Britain the pound collapsed. Shamefacedly, the British and French packed their bags and left.

Aftermath

For Britain the climb-down had been embarrassing. Eden never recovered and after a period of ill health resigned from office. The Suez Affair saw the sun sink on Britain's role in the Middle East. The affair also brought an Arab backlash. Arab states denounced the West and looked to Russia for support. Despite military defeat,

A Punch cartoon, November 1956. Identify the people in the cartoon and explain the cartoonist's view of the Suez Affair

Nasser emerged stronger and more popular than ever. Finally, Israel had put a stop to the fedayeen raids, although this problem would flare up again. To dampen tension on the Egypt–Israel border, a United Nations Emergency Force (UNEF) was sent into Sinai.

Using the evidence: the Sèvres accord

At the time of Suez, Eden vigorously denied any collusion (planning in secret) with France and Israel.

A *What we did do was to take 'police action' at once. Action to end the fighting and separate the armies.*
Sir Anthony Eden, Conservative Prime Minister, BBC broadcast, 3 November 1956

B *I have never believed the rather crude version of collusion between Britain, France and Israel.*
Colonel Wigg, Labour MP, speaking in the House of Commons, December 1958

Pineau: French Foreign Minister

Mollet: French Prime Minister

Ben-Gurion: Israeli Prime Minister

C *The Sèvres accord, Pineau told me, ran to three pages. At Eden's insistence one of its provisions was that it was never to be made public. The three copies, one each for Eden, Mollet and Ben-Gurion, were not to go into state archives that would one day be accessible to historians.*
Kennett Love: *Suez, The Twice Fought War*, 1969

D *The first substantial leaks happened in 1964 with the publication of three books....They were Finer's* Dulles over Suez, *Azeau's* Le Piège de Suez *and Bar Zohar's* Suez Ultra Secret....
France's Foreign Secretary, M. Pineau, was the source of the leak. He [related] the story of French collusion and British involvement to the American ambassador in Paris, and it was on Eisenhower's desk on November 2 [1956]. He also gave some facts off the record to our three authors. Then, provoked beyond measure by British evasions and untruths, he disclosed much of the story on BBC in July 1966.
E. Monroe: *Britain's Moment in the Middle East 1914–71*, 1981

1 How did Eden deceive the nation in source **A**? Why may he have done this?

2 How does source **B** support source **A**?

3 Study source **C**. How did Eden try to ensure that the Sèvres meeting remained secret? Why do you think he did this?

4 a) In what ways do sources C and D explain how the Sèvres meeting became known to historians?
   b) Sources C and D are written by modern historians. How may they be better placed to write about the Suez Affair than people involved at the time (source B)?

5 Cabinet papers remain secret for 30 years. Why was January 1987 of especial interest to historians of the Suez Affair?

The Six Day War

On 21 May 1967 Cairo Radio issued a warning to the people of Israel:

barrack: building in which soldiers are lodged

The Zionist barrack in Palestine is about to collapse and be destroyed. Every one of the hundred million Arabs has been living for the past nineteen years on one hope — to live to see the day Israel is liquidated.

It seemed that 11 years on from Suez the fragile peace that had existed between Israel and its Arab neighbours was about to be broken again. How had this come about? What had happened in the intervening years that would lead the Arabs and Israelis into their third major conflict?

Despite Nasser's defeat in the Suez War, he had emerged as the dominant personality of the Arab world. In an attempt to unite the Arab states, Egypt and Syria came together to form the United Arab Republic, but the union lasted for only two years because there were divisions among the Arabs. The one thing that Arabs had in common, however, was their hatred of Israel. This view intensified when Israel diverted the River Jordan in 1962 to irrigate the Negev Desert. Jordan complained bitterly that this was a violation of their territorial water.

In an attempt to achieve some unity, a summit meeting of Arab states convened in January 1964. One outcome was the formation of the Palestine Liberation Organisation (PLO), whose main aim was to free their homeland. Throughout 1965 and 1966 its military arm, Al-Assifa, based mainly in Syria, attacked Israeli settlements and spread terror. Israel countered with reprisal raids into Syria. A full-scale war seemed likely. Syria needed an ally and in November 1966 signed a defence pact with Egypt. Nevertheless, tension mounted in the first months of 1967 as the cross-border raids continued. Syrian guns targeted on northern Israel continually shelled Israeli settlements from the Golan Heights. On 7 April 1967, after four hours of Syrian shellfire, Israel launched a massive reprisal raid. Israeli jets silenced the Syrian guns, shot down six of their MiG fighters, and flew on to Damascus where they circled menacingly.

Backed by Russian intelligence, Nasser was now convinced of Israel's intention to attack Syria. Both Syria and Jordan were chiding him for his lack of action, and he wanted to reassert his authority. On 16 May 1967 he ordered a withdrawal of the blue-bereted UNEF, which had been in Sinai since 1956. As they left, the Egyptian army moved in. At the same time Cairo Radio unleashed a tirade of anti-Israeli propaganda which stirred up a hysterical fever of expectancy among the Arabs. On 22 May, Nasser raised the stakes considerably by blockading the Gulf of Aqaba, thus sealing off Israeli shipping from the Straits of Tiran. In Israeli eyes this was tantamount to a declaration of war. When King Hussein of Jordan flew to Egypt on 30 May to conclude a defence treaty, the writing was on the wall. Israel mobilised its forces and prepared for war. Would Nasser attack? In the event Nasser's intentions would count for little.

Blitzkrieg!

At 7.45 a.m. on 5 June 1967 Israeli Mirage jets launched a surprise attack on Egyptian air bases. Flying low and maintaining strict radio silence, they destroyed Egyptian airfields and aeroplanes. Later that day another wave of Israeli jets knocked out the Jordanian, Syrian and Iraqi Air Forces. Although only one day old, the war was virtually over. With the Egyptian Air Force knocked out, Israeli land forces swept across the Sinai Desert. As Egyptian troops retreated they were ensnared at the Mitla Pass, where they were bombed by Israeli planes. Within six days Egyptian troops had been pushed back to the Suez Canal.

Elsewhere the Israelis met with the same stunning success. The West Bank and Jerusalem were taken from Jordan. At the Wailing Wall, Defence Minister Moshe Dayan exclaimed: 'We have returned home to this most sacred of shrines never to part from it again.' On the northern front Israel seized the Golan Heights from Syria. By 10 June the Arabs stood defeated and demoralised. For Israel the war had been a spectacular success. It had acquired more than 70 000

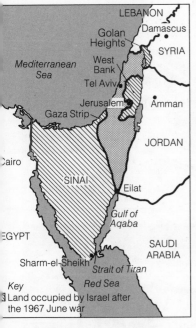

Right: *On the Mount of Olives, Israeli troops look out over the old city of Jerusalem before it is stormed and taken during the Six Day War*

square kilometres of territory and now had defensible borders. On the debit side, however, about 350 000 new refugees were created and Israel had to deal with the problem of governing another million Arabs (see map on page 45).

Using the evidence: Arab propaganda

The origins of the Six Day War in 1967 have aroused much controversy. Arabs say that Nasser never intended to invade. The Israelis say that they were right to strike first because all the signs were that Nasser would invade.

A Some cartoons that appeared in Arab newspapers in the month prior to the war.

(i) From the Egyptian daily paper *Al Massa*

(ii) From the Arab newspaper *Al-Jumhuriya*, 26 May 1967 (left)

(iii) From the Lebanese daily paper *Al-Jarida*, 31 May 1967 (below)

(iv) From the Lebanese daily paper *Al-Khayat*, 31 May 1967 (right)

B *The problem presently before the Arab countries is not whether the port of Eilat should be blockaded or how to blockade it – but how totally to exterminate the State of Israel for all time.*

President Nasser in an address to the Egyptian Parliament, 25 May 1967

C   *It is our chance, Arabs, to direct a blow of death and*
    annihilation to Israel and all its presence in our Holy Land. It
    is war for which we are waiting and in which we shall triumph.
                    Cairo Radio, 'Voice of the Arabs', 20 May 1967

D   *A special study ought to be devoted to the responsibility of*
    Cairo Radio for the disaster which overtook Egypt in 1967;
    this sort of propaganda was both the source of Nasserism's
    strength and its weakness. Some of this was realised after the
    military defeat. 'We have been saying things,' Al-Mussawar
    claimed, 'that we did not always mean . . . .' [But] . . . its main
    influence was on the Arabs; it raised their expectations to a
    point where the promises had to be fulfilled.
                    Walter Laquer: *The Road To War,* 1967

1   What are each of the cartoonists in source **A** trying to show?
    What do the cartoons all have in common?

2   a) How far do sources **A**, **B** and **C** prove that Nasser intended
        to invade?
    b) Apart from studying these sources, what else might a
        historian do in attempting to assess Nasser's intentions?

3   Study source **D**. What do you think is meant by the idea that
    'this sort of propaganda was both the source of Nasserism's
    strength and its weakness'?

4   Discuss the view that Arab propaganda made war bound to
    happen.

Following the shattering defeat in the Six Day War, the Arab states
met in Khartoum in August 1967. Here they decided there would be
'no peace, no recognition and no negotiation' with Israel. The Arab
struggle would continue. They gained some hope in November 1967
when the United Nations passed resolution 242 which called for:

1   The withdrawal of Israel from the occupied territories.
2   All Middle East states to live in peace within secure and
    recognised boundaries.
3   A just settlement to the refugee problem.

Nasser and King Hussein accepted these proposals. Israel, however,
refused to withdraw from the occupied territories unless the Arab
states recognised Israel's right to exist. Conflict flared again in 1968
when Egypt confronted Israel in a 'War of Attrition'. Artillery duels
across the Suez Canal caused many deaths. Both sides were flagging
by the time Nasser died in September 1970. Shortly before his death
Nasser had appointed the relatively unknown Anwar Sadat as Vice
President.

6 THE PALESTINIANS

Palestinians refer to the events of 1948–9 as 'The Catastrophe'. The British decision to renege on its Mandate, the bitter occupation of their villages by Zionist forces, and the final flight from their homeland are events of great sadness and deep humiliation to Palestinians. It is estimated that 700 000 Palestinians fled to surrounding Arab states where they settled in refugee camps. Jonathan Dimbleby described the camps:

> The conditions in the camps were atrocious. Families huddled bleakly in overcrowded tents. They were without adequate food or sanitation. When it rained, the narrow paths along each neat row were churned into a quagmire. The mud oozed into the tents. They lived in sodden clothes and slept in wet blankets. Influenza and pneumonia reached epidemic proportions. The young and old perished. Malnourished children were too weak to resist, and the old, left with no purpose, lacked the will.
>
> Even after rudimentary order had been imposed upon the camps, the conditions remained barbaric and degrading. Over the months, and into the years, the tents began to rot. They were discarded in favour of huts whose barrack rooms were often occupied by six or more families, sixty men, women and children, crowded together with only hanging blankets to offer privacy. They cooked, ate, washed and slept in public. Parents with many children could find no space in which to rest their exhausted bodies.
>
> J. Dimbleby: *The Palestinians*, 1979

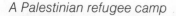
A Palestinian refugee camp

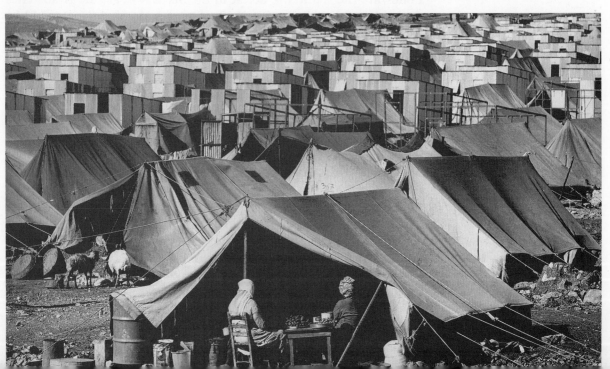

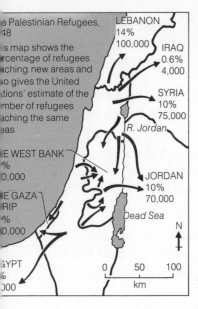

The map shows the percentage of refugees reaching new areas and also gives the United Nations' estimate of the number of refugees reaching the same areas

Palestinian Refugees, 48

LEBANON 14% 100,000

IRAQ 0.6% 4,000

SYRIA 10% 75,000

R. Jordan

THE WEST BANK % 0,000

JORDAN 10% 70,000

Dead Sea

N

THE GAZA STRIP % 0,000

EGYPT % 000

0   50   100
km

Under such conditions the refugees vegetated. It was not just the physical deprivation. The camps in the Gaza Strip were strictly controlled by the Egyptian authorities. Abu Jihad, now a leading member of the PLO, recalls his youth:

A *. . . the refugee camps in Gaza were prisons. And it was the same situation in the camps in Jordan, in Syria, in Iraq and in the Lebanon. Our people in the camps were totally isolated. They were not allowed any freedom of movement. They were not allowed to speak or write any word about our problem. They were not allowed to organise. They were not allowed to demonstrate. And those of us who did try to organise were treated as spies. I could tell you hundreds of stories about how all the Arab intelligence services intimidated and tortured our people in order to have their agents among us.*
Quoted in Alan Hart's book, *Arafat, Terrorist or Peacemaker?*
1985

Caged in the camps, the Palestinians grew bitter and frustrated. The world ignored their plight. Their Arab brothers, too, seemed intent on muzzling their identity. Nasser told the Palestinians to wait and be patient. Their best hope of returning to Palestine was through Arab unity. But little seemed to happen. Young Palestinians such as Yasser Arafat and Abu Jihad realised that it was up to Palestinians themselves to do something about their plight:

B *So we began to realise that we should organise independently; that this was the only way to return. We were forbidden, of course, to do this openly. It was a crime to assert our Palestinian identity, even in those countries which indulged in much posturing on our behalf. We were unable to organise in any way. . . .To say in*

Above: *Abu Jihad*

Right: *Yasser Arafat*

public 'We want to return home' or 'The Arabs are the cause of our misery' was to invite the severest reprisals. So we could draw only one conclusion: that we should work in secret to organise ourselves into a resistance movement.

Abu Jihad, quoted in Jonathan Dimbleby's book,
The Palestinians, 1979

In 1957 Yasser Arafat and Abu Jihad moved from Cairo to Kuwait. Here they formed the Palestine National Liberation Movement, called Fatah. In 1959 the first edition of a monthly magazine, *Our Palestine*, was published in Beirut. Its aim was to 'call to life' the Palestinians and to reaffirm their identity. Its language was bitter:

C *Where are you, dispersed people...where? Are you just flotsam, just jetsam strewn around.... How do you live? What's become of you? Are you living with your kith and kin, or are you scattered far and wide?*

Have you grown rich, children of the Catastrophe, or are you still dragging out the years in the shadow of hunger and sickness?

Our Palestine (Falastinuna), January 1964

To Palestinians, the loss of their land was deeply humiliating:

D *Our fundamental desire is for the land, the land which is ours, whose loss we deem...a national dishonour, a badge of ignominy and shame. Our land is our honour.... If that is taken from us, then everything goes.*

Our Palestine, January 1961

In the refugee camps Palestinians answered the call. The idea of The Return dominated camp life. Armed violence against the Israelis would be a necessary part of the struggle. Daily, Palestinian school children chanted the oath:

Palestine is our country
Our aim is to return
Death does not frighten us
Palestine is ours
We shall never forget her.
Another homeland we shall never accept!
Our Palestine, witness, O God and History
We promise to shed our blood for you!

Palestinian poetry, too, expressed ideas of The Return:

Beliefs such as these inspired the Fatah fighters who carried out the cross-border raids into Israel in 1965−7 (see Chapter 5).

The refugees are ever kindling,
In their camps, in that world of darkness,
The embers of revolt,
Gathering force, for the return
Their stolen rights cry in their hearts
Inflamed by misery and hunger.

E Dispersed, dispossessed and homeless, the Palestinians were forced to live in squalid refugee camps in neighbouring Arab states.

Questions

1   Abu Jihad is a leading member of the PLO and therefore a politically committed person. With reference to sources **A** and **B**, discuss the view that anything he writes is automatically biased.

2   Study the extracts from *Our Palestine* (sources **C** and **D**).
    a) Pick out words or phrases which reflect the bias of the author.
    b) Discuss the view that biased sources such as these are of little use to the historian.

3   a) With reference to source **E**, discuss the view that since the camera cannot lie, photographs are of more use than drawings to the historian.
    b) In what way may captions affect the way visual information is interpreted? Change the caption of **E** to alter the interpretation. Think how Israeli propagandists might caption the photograph.
    c) Look again at source **E**. Describe three ways in which the photographer has captured the plight of the Palestinians in exile.

A Palestinian women's liberation poster. In Palestinian symbolism the women usually fight for peace and the men for justice. What do you think is the message of the poster? Write your own caption

Fedayeen fighters

'To be or not to be'

The Six Day War of June 1967 was a crushing blow to the Arab world, yet Palestinians were in no mood to give up the struggle. As one Palestinian remarked: 'What choice is there for the Palestinians? To be or not to be, that is the question.' In the 'occupied territory' of the West Bank, Fatah resistance cells were organised. From bases in Jordan, Fatah launched guerilla attacks into Israeli territory. Salah Tamari, a Fatah fighter, recalls this period:

> *In 1967 in the West Bank, for the first time in my life I felt that I was a real human being. I had a gun in my hand. Between June 1967 and March 1968, I crossed into occupied territory thirty-five times. We always went across the Jordan....The fighters of that time were great men. They represented my ideal. They were honourable men who loved their country and wanted it back. We were isolated, lonely, but full of pride....*
>
> *It was a strange experience to be hiding in my own country. I felt both free and besieged. We were not just guerillas. We were doing what others thought impossible. We were always being advised to withdraw and we said, 'We will stand and fight'. We always wanted to be in direct contact with the enemy, to stand up and face the Israelis in the open.*

Quoted in Jonathan Dimbleby's book, *The Palestinians*, 1979

Following the 1967 war, Fatah's plan was essentially simple. Palestinian guerilla activity, mainly from Jordan, would draw Arab states into a wider conflict in which Israel would be annihilated.

On 21 March 1968 it appeared that the tactic might work. At dawn, 15 000 Israeli troops advanced on Karameh, a Palestinian

*King Hussein of Jordan
(seated)*

refugee town and guerilla base in Jordan. Instead of the usual guerilla ploy of vanishing to the hills, the Palestinian fighters resisted in open battle. In an unusual show of support for the Palestinians, King Hussein committed some of his forces to the defence of Karameh. Despite Israel's military superiority the Palestinians fought bravely and heroically. Their losses were heavy but when news spread of the courageous stand at Karameh, Fatah centres throughout the Arab world were besieged with new recruits. For the Palestinians Karameh was their finest hour.

After Karameh fedayeen activity increased. Its numbers rose from 300 in 1967 to 30 000 by 1970. Raids into Israel became commonplace. Israeli settlements were shelled, army patrols attacked, pipelines and railways blown up. In Tel Aviv and Jerusalem bombs were detonated in the market places.

This growth in guerilla activity alarmed King Hussein. He feared that the Palestinians were in danger of overrunning his country. In Amman, capital of Jordan, Palestinians paraded openly. Yasser Arafat, by now head of the PLO, tried to control his fighters but there were some Palestinian groups that operated outside his authority. One such group was the Popular Front for the Liberation of Palestine (PFLP), formed by Dr George Habash in 1967. The PFLP believed in more extreme methods. A number of daring international hijacks were carried out. Many innocent civilians died and sympathy for the Palestinian cause was lost. In one spectacular hijack three airliners, American, British and Swiss, were forced down at Dawson's Field in remote East Jordan. When negotiations failed, the hijackers blew up the aircraft as the world's television networks screened the drama.

For King Hussein this was the final straw. On 17 September 1970 he unleashed the Jordanian army on the Palestinians. There followed a fierce, bloody battle lasting ten days, from which the Jordanians emerged victorious. Hussein had kicked out the troublesome Palestinian fighters who were now forced to relocate their bases in Lebanon.

Assignment

The date is October 1970. Imagine you are a Western news reporter assigned to conduct an interview with a Fatah fighter such as Salah Tamari. You want to find out:

a) Why he decided to fight.
b) Whether he regards himself as a terrorist.
c) What it feels like to go on a raid and how he feels when innocent people are killed.
d) What he hopes to achieve.
e) His view of other Arab states.

Now write out your interview in full.

WAR AND PEACE

When Anwar Sadat took over as President of Egypt in October 1970 following Nasser's death, Egyptians began to tell humorous stories. One went:

> *Shortly after Nasser's death a Cairo taxi driver took his country cousin on his first tour of the city. Stopping at a café in a populous quarter the cousin saw a big picture of the 'immortal leader' [Nasser] shaking hands with his successor. 'Ah,' he sighed, 'our beloved Nasser...God rest his soul. But who is that with him?' Not himself recognising Sadat, but eager to demonstrate his sophistication, the taxi driver replied... 'Oh, that's the owner of the café.'*
>
> David Hirst and Irene Beeson, *Sadat*, 1981

It seemed that Nasser would be a hard act to follow. One way in which Sadat hoped to consolidate his leadership was to regain the area of Sinai which Egypt had lost in the 1967 war. Israel, however, still faced the Egyptians across the Suez Canal in a tense situation of 'no war, no peace'. Sadat hoped to break the deadlock. 1971, he proclaimed, would be his year of decision: 'We shall not allow 1971 to pass without deciding the issue, whether through peace or war — even if it means sacrificing one million lives.' 1971 passed and no decision was made. The Egyptian people grew restless. In 1972 Sadat sent home 17 000 Russian military and political advisers. This move was popular with many Egyptians who wished to rid themselves of Russian interference. Sadat hoped that the Americans would be sufficiently impressed to help Egypt negotiate a peace settlement with Israel. In the end it yielded nothing. Sadat's standing was rock bottom when he made a speech in Cairo on 28 September 1973:

> *We have had enough of words...we know our goal and we are determined to reach it...the liberation of our territory is the fundamental task before us....*

Egyptians paid little attention. Why should they? The empty boasts had all been heard before. No one, including the Israelis, took Sadat seriously any more. Few realised that Egypt and Syria had secretly been planning war. The date, 6 October — the day of the Jewish holiday of Yom Kippur, when Israeli life comes to a standstill — had already been fixed.

The Yom Kippur War

On 6 October 1973 Egyptian forces broke through the Israeli defensive wall, the Bar Lev Line, in three sectors and took up positions

October 1973, in the town of Suez. The cease-fire line between Israel and Egypt is marked by the width of the road with a United Nations post to one side

in Sinai. At the same time 500 Syrian tanks launched an attack on Israeli-held positions in the Golan Heights. This time the Israelis were caught napping. They took 72 hours to mobilise and when they did begin to counterattack they found another nasty surprise waiting for them. The Egyptians were armed with Soviet-built bazookas, anti-tank 'suitcase' missiles and the portable SAM 7 (surface to air) missiles. In time, however, the Israelis recovered. On 12 October they hit back against Syria and regained the Golan Heights. On 15 October the Israeli general, Ariel Sharon, made a bold push across the Suez Canal, establishing a bridgehead on the west bank. By the time the UN-sponsored cease-fire came on 24 October both sides could claim victory, yet both had suffered damage.

During the war there had been some dangerous moments. Both superpowers had intervened to supply their client states. At the height of the conflict it appeared that both Russia and the United States might become directly involved.

In the course of the war the Arabs deployed a new weapon: the oil weapon. The Organisation of Petroleum-Exporting Countries (OPEC) met and agreed to cut oil production by five per cent per month until Israel withdrew. Saudi Arabia placed a total ban on exports to the United States and cut production by ten per cent. The price of oil rose dramatically and exposed a raw nerve in Western economies. The Arabs became aware of their potential economic power.

Despite an inconclusive military outcome, Sadat had come out of the war with much credit. He had restored Egyptian pride and shown the Arab world that the Israelis were not unbeatable. Above all, Sadat had broken the stalemate of 'no peace, no war' with Israel.

After the war Dr Henry Kissinger, the US Secretary of State, bustled energetically around the capitals of the Middle East in search of a peaceful settlement. Eventually Israel and Egypt entered into negotiations which led to the return of Sinai to Egypt in 1982. The following table shows the major milestones on the 'road to peace'.

The road to peace	
January 1974	Dr Kissinger began his 'shuttle diplomacy' and was successful in securing troop disengagements between Israel and Egypt. In June, Kissinger negotiated a similar agreement with Syria.
June 1975	Egypt reopened the Suez Canal after Israel withdrew her troops from the canal zone.
November 1977	President Sadat took the bold step of going to Jerusalem where he addressed the Knesset (the Israeli Parliament). He told them: 'We welcome you to live among us in peace and security.' Sadat offered 'borders secure against aggression'. Begin (Prime Minister of Israel) responded by stating his wish for 'real peace, involving full reconciliation between the Jewish and Arab nations'. In December Begin visited Egypt.
September 1978	Negotiations proved long and arduous. When the peace process faltered, the US President, Jimmy Carter, stepped in and invited Sadat and Begin to his holiday lodge at Camp David. Two agreements were reached as a basis for peace: 1 An Israeli-Egyptian Peace. In return for Israeli recognition and security Egypt would regain all its territory in Sinai. The Israeli withdrawal would be phased. 2 A Framework for Peace in the Middle East. This was an attempt to address the Palestinian question. Palestinians living on the West Bank and Gaza Strip would gain self-governing status.
March 1979	Sadat and Begin signed a peace treaty in Washington. Both agreed to recognise 'each other's right to live in peace within secure and recognised boundaries'. The Palestine question, however, remained an unsolved problem. The treaty was denounced by other Arab states who accused Sadat of selling out to the Israelis.
October 1981	Sadat was assassinated by Muslim extremists. Hosni Mubarak took over as President.
April 1982	The last Israeli soldier and civilian left Sinai. The Israeli withdrawal was complete.

Using the evidence: reactions to the Israeli-Egyptian peace treaty

A   A cartoon from the Saudi newspaper *Al-Riyadh*, 30 August 1980.

B   In Baghdad, Sadat is hanged in effigy as Iraqis demonstrate after the signing of the Israeli–Egyptian Peace Treaty.

C   The peacemakers – the signing of the Israeli–Egyptian Peace Treaty, March 1979.

1 The writing on the sword in source **A** says 'Camp David'. What is happening in this cartoon? Explain the significance of what Sadat is wearing on his head and holding in his left hand.

2 How do sources **A** and **B** help to explain the reaction of some Arabs to the Camp David agreements? Why do you think some Arab states reacted in this way?

3 Identify the three people shown in source **C**. How and why does their reaction differ from that of the cartoonist (source **A**) and the people in the other photograph (source **B**)?

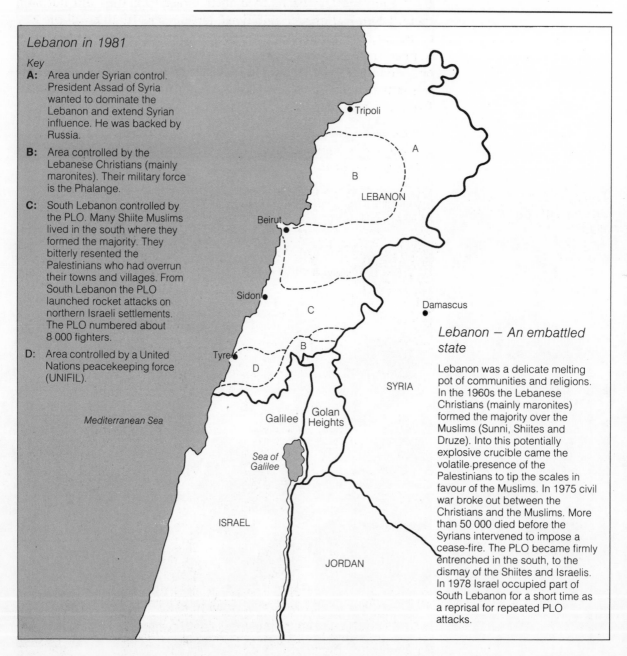

Lebanon in 1981

Key

A: Area under Syrian control. President Assad of Syria wanted to dominate the Lebanon and extend Syrian influence. He was backed by Russia.

B: Area controlled by the Lebanese Christians (mainly maronites). Their military force is the Phalange.

C: South Lebanon controlled by the PLO. Many Shiite Muslims lived in the south where they formed the majority. They bitterly resented the Palestinians who had overrun their towns and villages. From South Lebanon the PLO launched rocket attacks on northern Israeli settlements. The PLO numbered about 8 000 fighters.

D: Area controlled by a United Nations peacekeeping force (UNIFIL).

Mediterranean Sea

Tripoli

A

B

LEBANON

Beirut

Sidon

Damascus

C

B

Tyre

D

SYRIA

Galilee | Golan Heights

Sea of Galilee

ISRAEL

JORDAN

Lebanon — An embattled state

Lebanon was a delicate melting pot of communities and religions. In the 1960s the Lebanese Christians (mainly maronites) formed the majority over the Muslims (Sunni, Shiites and Druze). Into this potentially explosive crucible came the volatile presence of the Palestinians to tip the scales in favour of the Muslims. In 1975 civil war broke out between the Christians and the Muslims. More than 50 000 died before the Syrians intervened to impose a cease-fire. The PLO became firmly entrenched in the south, to the dismay of the Shiites and Israelis. In 1978 Israel occupied part of South Lebanon for a short time as a reprisal for repeated PLO attacks.

Round 5: Israel invades Lebanon

On 6 June 1982 the Israeli army invaded Lebanon. For the past decade Israel's northern settlements had faced constant shelling and guerilla attacks by PLO fighters operating from Lebanon (see map on page 58). Now Begin declared his intention:

...to push back the terrorists to a distance of 40 kilometres to the north so that all our civilians in the region of Galilee will be set free of the permanent threat on their lives.

By 7 June the Israelis reached their target. But they did not stop there. Begin had greater ambitions. Israeli tanks rumbled all the way to Beirut, the capital, so that by 10 June the PLO fighters were trapped in the city. It seemed that Begin wanted to crush the PLO once and for all. The lightning speed of the Israeli advance, however, was only made possible by using the tactic of massive bombardment. Even in Israel such methods caused concern:

The heavy bombardments, the enormous destruction and the high number of casualties among the refugees and the Lebanese population were supposed to make it easier for the Israeli Army to occupy

A refugee camp in South Lebanon, after an Israeli attack

the area with a low number of casualties. Thus an immoral act was done: in order to lessen the number of our casualties our government was prepared to cause heavy casualties on the other side, including civilians, even Lebanese, who are not a party to the war between Israel and the Palestinians.

Professor Porath, writing in *Ha'aretz*, an Israeli newspaper, June 1982

With its vast firepower and military hardware the Israeli army brought death and destruction to the ravaged towns of Lebanon. The Israelis also used a range of frightening terror weapons. Phosphorous shells, restricted to open battlefields by a 1980 UN convention, were fired into Beirut. The effects were devastating:

Dr Shamaa found that the two five-day-old twins had already died. But they were still on fire. 'I had to take the babies and put them in buckets of water to put out the flames,' she said. 'When I took them out half an hour later they were still burning. Even in the mortuary they smouldered for hours.'

Robert Fisk, *The Times*, July 1982

After several weeks such indiscriminate attacks eventually rooted out the PLO fighters who were besieged in West Beirut. Under the eye of an American-led international peacekeeping force, the PLO were evacuated and dispersed throughout the Arab world.

As the PLO left, Israeli forces moved in and took up positions around the Palestinian refugee camps of Sabra and Chatila. No one could get in or out of the camps without Israeli approval. At about 6 p.m. on Thursday 16 September, Christian Phalangists, allies of the Israelis and hated enemies of the Muslim Palestinians, entered the camps. War journalists were not allowed in until the Saturday. When they went in they found an appalling massacre had taken place.

...the victims were men, women and children of all ages, from the very old to the very young, even babes in arms. They were killed in every possible way. The lucky ones were shot, singly or in groups. Others were strangled or had their throats slit. They were mutilated, before or after death; genitals and breasts were sliced off; some had crosses carved on their chests, a Phalangist trademark.

Michael Jansen, *The Battle of Beirut*, 1982

Initially, Begin rejected as 'blood libel' any Israeli responsibility. Later, in Israel, the Kahan Commission of Inquiry found the Israelis in charge of the operation, Begin, Sharon and Eitan, 'indirectly responsible' for not taking 'energetic and immediate actions' to prevent the massacre. Sabra and Chatila shocked and outraged the world and brought further condemnation of Israel's conduct in Lebanon.

The Shiite Muslims

On 10 April 1985 a pretty 16-year-old Lebanese schoolgirl named Sana Mhaydali climbed into a white Peugeot 504 packed with 440lbs of TNT. She drove up to an Israeli convoy. When two Israeli soldiers approached her, Sana detonated the bomb. The two soldiers were killed outright, another two lay injured, and Sana was blown to bits.

Sana Mhaydali, as she appeared on Lebanese television after her suicide. In a pre-recorded interview, she said: 'I chose death in order to fulfil my national duty.'

Many in the West found Sana's suicide hard to understand. To fellow Shiites, however, she died a heroine. Many queued to follow her. For Shiites like Sana, inspired by Ayatollah Khomeini's Islamic fundamentalism (the strictest form of the Islamic faith), martyrdom is the ultimate glory. As one Shiite explained: 'You wait to die of old age. We choose to die for Allah, and Allah will reward us for dying for his cause.'

To Israelis the Shiites represented a new and, in some ways, more frightening enemy than the Palestinians. Yet when Israel invaded Lebanon in 1982 the Shiites had first welcomed them as liberators with rice and garlands of flowers. For more than a decade the Palestinians had dominated the Shiites in South Lebanon. When the Shiites wanted their villages back, however, the Israelis refused to go home. Soon the Shiites became embroiled in the Israeli terror. Many of their people died. A resistance militia, Amal, was formed. Their targets have not only been the Israelis but their Christian allies, the South Lebanese Army (SLA) and the United States, who supported the Israeli presence in Lebanon by providing weapons. In October 1983 Amal carried out a terrifying suicide attack on a US marine base in which more than 200 Americans died.

The Israeli response to such attacks has been the policy of the 'Iron Fist'. Suspected resistance fighters are dragged out in the middle of the night for interrogation. Villages are bulldozed, suspects tortured.

Withdrawal

Under the constant threat to their lives the morale of the Israeli army sagged. Many Israelis openly questioned the conduct and continuing presence of their army in Lebanon. In the summer of 1985 Israel finally withdrew from Lebanon, although a significant number of Israeli 'advisers' stayed behind to assist their allies, the SLA. Nevertheless, occasional rocket attacks on Galilee began again. The situation in 1986 remained tense.

Peace and the Palestinians

In 1968 the Palestinians first formed their National Charter. They rejected the existence of Israel and called for an armed struggle, if necessary, to regain their land. In 1974 Yasser Arafat addressed the United Nations. He announced: 'Today I have come bearing an olive branch and a freedom fighter's gun. Do not let the olive branch fall from my hand.' In the decade that followed the olive branch withered. The gun ruled.

Since Camp David several peace initiatives to settle the Palestine question have failed. In February 1985 a joint Jordanian–Palestinian peace initiative was launched. Progress proved painfully slow. Israel refused to recognise the PLO, which it says is a terror organisation. Yet Arafat, head of the PLO, has the backing of most Palestinians and claims to be the sole legitimate representative of the Palestinian people. Until recently the PLO did not recognise Israel, but unofficial statements say they would be prepared to do so if the United States endorsed the right of Palestinians to 'self-determination'. In February 1986, however, the peace process broke down. A solution to the Palestine question seemed as far away as ever.

The peace process took place against a background of heightening international Palestinian terrorism and Israeli reprisal. In October 1985 the *Achille Lauro* liner was hijacked. Israel replied by bombing the PLO headquarters at Tunis. In December, Palestinian groups sprayed the airports at Rome and Vienna with bullets. The PLO rejected responsibility for these attacks, which were thought to be the work of the extremist Abu Nidal faction based in Libya. United States President, Ronald Reagan, claimed Libya was a hornet's nest of Palestinian terrorist groups. The Libyan leader, Colonel Qadhafi, was denounced as public enemy number one and the United States bombed Libya. Undoubtedly this spate of terrorism and reprisal hindered the peace process. The gun still ruled in the Middle East. Yet without peace the long-term consequences could be unthinkable. Brian Urquhart, Under Secretary to four UN Secretary Generals and regarded as 'Mr Middle East', is pessimistic:

> *Arafat is right. We are on a course for catastrophe. Perhaps time has already run out. I fear that Arafat's contribution to the peace*

process will not be officially recognised until it is much too late — for him and all of us.

Quoted in Alan Hart's book, *Arafat, Terrorist or Peacemaker?*
1985

The danger is that moderates such as Arafat may be swept aside by Palestinian extremists.

A just solution to the Arab—Israeli conflict is perhaps the first item on any agenda of world problems.

Assignment: looking at the present in the context of the past

1 a) Describe the current nature of the Arab—Israeli conflict. Use the various media to examine the current situation of:
    (i) the Palestinian refugees
    (ii) Palestinian terrorism and Israeli reprisal
    (iii) the PLO
    (iv) the peace process.
   b) Can you detect any bias in the way the Western media reports the Arab—Israeli conflict?

2 Explain how the Arab—Israeli conflict developed from a small, local conflict at the beginning of the twentieth century to one of global dimensions. Consider carefully the following 'turning points':
    (i) The Balfour Declaration (Chapter 2)
    (ii) The rise of Hitler (Chapter 3)
    (iii) The Arab Rebellion, 1936—9 (Chapter 4)
    (iv) The UN partition of Palestine, 1947 (Chapter 4)
    (v) The Suez Affair, 1956 (Chapter 5)
    (vi) The Six Day War, 1967 (Chapter 5)
    (vii) The Yom Kippur War and the importance of oil (Chapter 7)
    (viii) Palestinian resistance (Chapters 6 and 7)

3 Take one of the events listed above and explain how Palestinians and Israelis might view the event differently.

4 What is your view of the Arab—Israeli conflict? Should Israel exist? Do the Palestinians have a right to a homeland?

5 Why is a settlement of the Arab—Israeli conflict so important? What solution to the conflict would you propose? (You may draw a map to help explain your proposal if you wish.)

INDEX

Numerals in **bold** denote illustrations